I MADE
rich
YOU A NEW M
ard l.
ACHINE A
lucy
LL IT DO
s h y n
ES IS HOPE

```
the operating system print//document
```

I made for you a new machine and all it does is hope

ISBN: 978-1-946031-44-0
Library of Congress Control Number: 2018915123
copyright © 2019 Richard Lucyshyn
edited and designed by ELÆ [Lynne DeSilva-Johnson]
cover image by Richard Lucyshyn with art direction by Elæ

is released under a Creative Commons CC-BY-NC-ND (Attribution, Non Commercial, No Derivatives) License: its reproduction is encouraged for those who otherwise could not afford its purchase in the case of academic, personal, and other creative usage from which no profit will accrue.

Complete rules and restrictions are available at:
http://creativecommons.org/licenses/by-nc-nd/3.0/

For additional questions regarding reproduction, quotation, or to request a pdf for review contact: operator@theoperatingsystem.org

This text was set in Avenir, Minion, Franchise, and OCR-A Standard.

Books from The Operating System are distributed to the trade by SPD/Small Press Distribution and Ingram, with production by Spencer Printing, in Honesdale, PA, in the USA.

```
the operating system
```

www.theoperatingsystem.org
operator@theoperatingsystem.org

I made for you a new machine and all it does is hope

RICHARD LUCYSHYN

2018-19 OS System Operators

CREATIVE DIRECTOR/FOUNDER/MANAGING EDITOR: ELÆ
[Lynne DeSilva-Johnson]
DEPUTY EDITOR: Peter Milne Greiner
CONTRIBUTING EDITOR, EXPERIMENTAL SPECULATIVE POETICS:
Kenning JP Garcia
CONTRIBUTING EDITOR, FIELD NOTES: Adrian Silbernagel
CONTRIBUTING EDITOR, IN CORPORE SANO: Amanda Glassman
CONTRIBUTING EDITOR, GLOSSARIUM: Ashkan Eslami Fard
CONTRIBUTING EDITOR, GLOSSARIUM / RESOURCE COORDINATOR:
Bahaar Ahsan
JOURNEYHUMAN / SYSTEMS APPRENTICE: Anna Winham
DIGITAL CHAPBOOKS / POETRY MONTH COORDINATOR: Robert Balun
TYPOGRAPHY WRANGLER / DEVELOPMENT COORDINATOR: Zoe
Guttenplan
DESIGN ASSISTANTS: Lori Anderson Moseman, Orchid Tierney, Michael Flatt
SOCIAL SYSTEMS / HEALING TECH: Curtis Emery
VOLUNTEERS and/or ADVISORS: Adra Raine, Alexis Quinlan, Clarinda Mac
Low, Bill Considine, Careen Shannon, Joanna C. Valente, L. Ann Wheeler, Erick
Sáenz, Knar Gavin, Joe Cosmo Cogen, Sarah Dougherty

The Operating System is a member of the **Radical Open Access Collective**, a community of scholar-led, not-for-profit presses, journals and other open access projects. Now consisting of 40 members, we promote a progressive vision for open publishing in the humanities and social sciences.

Learn more at: http://radicaloa.disruptivemedia.org.uk/about/

Your donation makes our publications, platform and programs possible!
We <3 You.
http://www.theoperatingsystem.org/subscribe-join/

I made for you a new machine and all it does is hope

for Kelly & Hazel & Levon

contents

psallite sapienter	15
some poems	17
Gather your lessons & settle a heart	19
In the woods we build monuments to our different selves	20
Dread reckoning	21
ten thousand psalms	23
a plea	61
confiteor // untitled	65
some poems	89
Manmade water	91
The gospel writers	92
Unwritten & open letters to Jack Christian	93
Make or break Star City	94
Drumbelly gnosis	95
I made for you a new machine and all it does is hope	97
notes on the text	115
acknowledgements	116

> nor did I look at anything
> with no other light or guide
> than the one that burned in my heart.
>
> St. John of the Cross

psallite sapienter

say star and say sun // say halo   frost and feather // say branch
or bend // basalt   bite and schist // say taut and say tongue

tooth or tree // say mound beneath some other moon // say drift
and the differences of water // say always bright this newest heart

or also dark the river // say what you will witness and then become
say that wings unbreak the sky // say which cloud was always void

then wrap your limbs with wire // say ghost I love you and grieve
the last grievesome river // say the last shape we make is light

and your name's sharpest sigh from brighter lips // say the kiss
of sacred mouths again   again // say the map of hidden places

in your most secret atlas // say the book is on fire and a breath
is the spark // say sky   the sky   your undark heart being now

at rest // say what help you have and give // say faith out loud
say clavicytherium or shattered lion   lumen and the left hand

of tungsten // say *contempus* and whatever // *mundi* and else
the false and lonely testament of your nearest self // say yes

and say grace // say grace // say grace and hope to mean it

some poems

Gather your lessons & settle a heart

One is sorry. Two is joy. Others rhyme to every other
But what you are is slant. Maybe 40 crows are what
You are. The sound of a slippery hitch on fire is you.
We saw smoke and reckoned where's water and walked.
Adjacent to the line on a map that means fence is where
You said you'd wait but we watched and you didn't.
It was weird a little but we were pilgrims approximately
And used to unknowing. One time we went entire days
Without looking under any stones. A big lousy window
Is what you resemble. Mostly glass and dripping slow
But not without charm. In the hornbook of a shoeless
Child you are the scribble that stands for stomping.
We scratched your name on every puddle and when
There wasn't any water we climbed a tree and sang.

In the woods we built monuments to our different selves

What is a sound really. What is our body
and how are we also a place.

Instead of the river I found this gun.

I was looking for the beautiful name of something
and only found a circle of burning tires.

It was a flag something. It was a somehow statue
to a place in time that was our always body also.

It was one idea of nation building.

Other ideas happened sometimes. And then
they unhappened themselves slightly.

It goes like that. Mostly in the woods.

There is where the bodies are.

There and there and there is the where we are.

Dread reckoning

To stand beneath this tree is your penance.

Understand that for you the opposite smile can never be unmade which is your penance also.

Dust is your penance and water will scrape your tongue.

Your penance is shabby.

To be dirt. To be blood without time.

You will always hold dissonance and it will always be weird.

When you write your name some feature of your only face will be erased as penance.

Someone will fuck up your framework somehow constantly.

This will be known to a sort of grace.

Your penance will be grace. It is grace.

Your penance is grace.

ten thousand psalms

[psalm]

keep, love, the door of my lips   and for this lion
    weep   *selah*   my faults poured as cups unto

these, which lighted   so lent   little read from
some breviary of birds, *psallite*, o dearest heart

as your breath is knitted to mine, then unknow

[psalm]

would that we with every ask dried, other or yet soon
seek to   atone or be moondrunk and rung, as creek

could we be better   left of this marrowclenched why
glassed until knob and cry, a cloud or uncopper heart

to be again born, machined new   unsad, a sound for

[psalm]

an alder stroke, ambit of kneelers and locks
or the lede below a heart's hornbook, a saint

astragalus or nearer to beech, our lots cast
to bricks, a gamble we made and unmade

searching to grace, the oily residue of hope

[psalm]

unbend, you kneelers, for to shoeless meddle
this sand, robed by splinter and gust, for grain

these feet will be always unwashed, instead to
walk from end, the stride held as first principle

dusted *ad astra* or whatever meant as where

[psalm]

    beseech and yearn, the creek's plainsong   lusting craw
and yea, unhinder my tongue to touch as tendril this thigh

        as belly blessed by kiss, unvoiced among ten thousand
        chief to gaze, my sidelong hands placed a sun between

    of this part silver, o body o breast   lie these twin lillies

[psalm]

unseen ascend, without waking   still, this last dark
this secret ladder, by which is meant this lonesome

climb from sleep, through dream by waking to song
unsinging trumpets unspooled, to last a saintly rope

memory of coils become, at rest, my progress now

[psalm]

my brightest love, who suffers by twelve such stars
these dozen names for grace   cindered, from flag

collapse to ash, these throats joined   gutbound so
and too decry false all pain, or this again by just veil

bending hand   some latter dark, antiphon now sky

[psalm]

deliver me this untidy breath, joined by and bluster
pious filled or lightly same, now shunned, be prayer

but slow along, counterpoint with or cantered, cant
sung from pillowed breath, leg slung and sweated

you in tidy gasp   gamboled to twine, of tether or

[psalm]

whose breath unbreathed this deliberate stain
beneath and beneath and beyond, tautbound

spine   spiracle, these lines bothered by bone
sprung again from black, kiting the elder crease

here, *sum*   edged wind, a broken staff or I am

[psalm]

better to reckon on this doubt   these subtle nods to certain
blazed trails, *per pedes* unshod, so stumble an internal way

but hide your track beneath umber leaves   between ocher
and branch, where new logics are made to speak on the old

edges blurred, four steps or seven around, an empty pond

[psalm]

staunching, the supplicant tongue of fire in order to
or never done as once so held in hand, of morning

of fleecing wind, wing and the wingless memory of
upreached branches, how many faultless steps, or

in truth can you see, the sediment nature of home

[psalm]

being now at rest, limned   liminal and pulsing
the empty lantern or gullied shade, dark thrown

fractaled but not without pause, pattern lacked
a cuss defined by breadth but never breathing

between   sphered, the last dim space of null

[psalm]

skittered and sprung, erumpent lights   breezeblown
as spore   as seed, cast bright over rusty machines

capsid blind, or were we not yet endeared to walls
chancel and nave   or breathfilled aumbry at last

give unto me, dear friend, what is to bug and trash

[psalm]

tell me grace, say unto me tumble and leaf   seraph
the shake of horns upon the gate, what sounded to

a perfect knowledge, zephyr brown   blown to pass
as circles turn we so turn, trembling blue, cry jubilee

say ecstacy of text tooth, my unname spoke love

[psalm]

    eat this scroll, bless and be   but always barbed
     a copper heart   unwrapped, held hard to havoc

    spoken by chime, harvest and helmed but slant
     a red cord raveled, be to this lasting skein tied

it was weird how it was, our flags false in this light

[psalm]

a simple ravening, to place the good and final till
of mineral fields, grieve and unhand, friend, night

and damp, wrapped in rudding leaves like plaster
like blooded limbs, bent to bear the bearing weight

of winter   bound yet to the last machine of sun

[psalm]

   for the sake of augury, these branches   this creek
   in deference to feather and psalm, awoke on a hum

   some muddle of leaves   of green in duskdun water
   tremblefound by wetted tongue, taut unbellowed sky

   exalt and be sworn to skin   so too rootsong   unfall

[psalm]

what we ask, sweet angel, what to seek and what know
some new machine balmed smooth   fueled of hope

and ever to unbrine this blood, ours an always pulse
give clot these tears, daily find our fear   what heart

we pound from habit, wager memories we dare to hold

[psalm]

grackle or grouse, which bird garbage others called
in field or fence along, one thousand graceful things

you told in tongues, bashful from wing   unwinged
blacking feather bled, your lasting bones so with air

or filled by spark, orison of sound   tendon and claw

[psalm]

humble thy servant, at least thy servant notched
knelt by branch to fruited bloom, adjacent to null

with seven trumpets sound, to prepare and walk
faithlessly these blank trails, pass to new   yea

beloved, that which hath an ear this cry unheard

[psalm]

better from old and well hummed air, or trammeled by
from nature hewn, sundered, nightly drawn from tree

of tree become   beneath, of stygian thought drawn
like uprooted teeth, the valley a vault   cloister pined

this reredos of moonseed, cut to screen our pale offer

[psalm]

o you bellow and breath, breast   you trumpet   o
song transcribed by love, or gathered to canticle so

cleared to, o heart in the heart of the o spring heart
green and graced this unkept alley   of blooms for

these and to thee, o sweet cautery, your name sung

[psalm]

    neither have these two coats apiece   nor scree
    brittle bent, by talus   farrago of dust, which staff

    left behind and blown, green by moss shot through
    these epistrophic branches, *in pectore* and yet not

    this journey, my love, to tender with grace to the sky

[psalm]

by gull   by gale   by gutwing and gold throat
whoso steps upon these stones, this rusted

towerblown   vatic pulse of ordinary ramble
dew bleached and bonepale, as a sky creased

cast aside iron, wizened fierce   bent to grey

[psalm]

narthex or to nave, triforium bent as tree   branched
candlesworn and sparkleaf, this hung and hale censer

deliberate to a kind   a practiced stillness attended to
ad aeterno or *ab*, absolved in the sense of undressed

belly swelled   loosed, from burgundy shift to a seam

[psalm]

the queried or quarrelsome breath, bit from cloth
adamant as cowl or nothing so dissimilar as caul

white   bituminous, the warbling sense of hawk
lost in the red of how many scarlets, slab and grief

held out to a thrush   the most final spark of dare

[psalm]

instead of the vestiges of, it was scrabble and hardnose
skate or ray among the reeds, full drunk or dallygrown

a ply among same, these radical notions relative to
revered by, were convicted again by so many hands

of dust and thrum, which sound we pulsed to crows

[psalm]

again as this oblivion, *non sum*, my love, *sicut ceteri*
some angel   *homines*, give depth and call to blank

within these white halls, have we been again or ever
a faithful steward, *verbum salutis*   whatever craved

always we fell, *urbi et orbi*, our pace too slow for lift

[psalm]

    of temperate hue, bound between or easterly
of elderberry, or else elegy   else cloister of pine

a welter of disrobing thoughts, once transcribed
in the margins of, in lights   *in pectore* and light

these your breasts, allayed, a new genus of ache

[psalm]

kindred or kindly, the hindered climb to cause
sully bright and brine, blind by forest and fast

we only held what our hollow hand could holy trace
blessing the branch, gathered a choir from flight

a sharpened quill, feathers cut for lichen scrolls

[psalm]

forsobbed and justly sworn, it was me what it was
what killed these killed kids, what sidled   lapsed

and bent from sight, the world was always as fence
or else falter, some brownbled shadow left ignored

to blacken from scene alone, in my longest shame

[psalm]

more worked than working, some last possession of void unto
which I have my will given, withdrawn from darkness

from lack of notice to chancel, *peccavi et peccavi et* same
pulled to a thread, a goodness not begotten but redeemed

it makes and makes and makes again itself, it pours being

[psalm]

which one slid and sallied, which one made wise
or willed the weather to braid these loose limbs

or also falter the march, a detuned tattoo draggled
the snare   unrolled the flag, which, dearest heart

was held to station, what swallows blame is grief

[psalm]

grave or the grieving, the slipped knot is same
and underplaced a mitre   a rook, coiled there

a heaving mass of infinite grace, slanted to green
must we now heave our teeth to the sun, sweet

friend, believe, there is no only sound for hope

plea

and who am I, sister, to hazard
my hope could be of matter

beloved children, ever could I
to atone   could I even know
the full weight of such a sound

confiteor // untitled

it was me what killed these killed kids

    me what killed these

               these killed kids

        killed these killed

            these   kids

it was me

    me what killed

               these killed kids whose names I too stole

                    whose names too erased //

                whose names changed

                      too destroyed

it was me what broke the teeth

    me what   teeth

        these   kids

it was me what killed

it was me what killed

it was me

    me   these   kids

my bastard stride was such and bright / and thus unburned
it was me
>> who burned black // black burned / these bodies
>> > black   these kids
>> who burned   these killed kids
>> > the sun   every sun   another sun blacked

blacked and blacked again // and loud so bellowed
>> > > an illicit clan   moonlocked // unjudged
> I was false
> > false
> I was false and graceless burned

I was graceless   unbound // bellyfull

                             delivered whole and wet with caul

            and yes this sun // and too this light

                which sun by suffering borne

which breath aloft   which breath on fire // of fire

       breath by branch   by knot   by branch and knot

                           this knot

this knotted twine   held / so wound to length

                                                                                so thrown and caught

                                   so heaved and raised

                                       and raised

a risen wind pulled through / damp and dancing feet to sway

                                         these dancing feet till stone

                                               till stopped and stone

and then to straddle and piss the gardens

and then   these gardens untilled

blooded upon or bled // and bled

                               and bled these killed kids

and gasped a puddled psalm of lasting havoc

                                 of   havoc sprung over // eternal

it was me / this garden where of rape become

                        of rape I made

from lust a bright pain birthed

such sprawl and shine / these tongues gathered and jarred

                        these tongues unloosed by dark

it was me

and yes me   again   what wrote hate   hate wrote
    was me who ledgered numbers for names
and   me   what columned these accounts
                                    these sums
untruth tallied by lasting breath

it was again me what scrawled slave // chattel and so

how many backs I tore / it was me what 39 lashed

                                                what held the whip

                     was me

                                       what turned away

                   was me

whose blooded lips   whose falsing tongue

                   was me

it was me what eyes closed / my eyes which   blind from

and yet so blind // and thus blacked

what rent the sky of grace

what broke such bones

                        to fill the sea

was me that drowned from fear

    me   from faith

and me that fell to graves // and thus felled

was me what turned to final grieve / palms by tremor raised

// or coins wrapped in dust

it was mine

    my blooded heart // these and these killed

these killed kids

it was me what damned my own heart

my heart that beats my untidy heart my heart
which tore itself from grace my heart put low
my heart which bleeds and bled and craved
to bleed to swallow the last blood of my heart
my hollow heart which yearned my plundered
heart my heart which walked away my heart
denied from light my burdened heart that slept
while my heart was crushed my callow heart
my coward heart that hates my hated heart
unsworn but cowed my yielding heart below
the muck my burning heart my sinning heart
my sweated heart of null my heart that begs
my heart of thieves my trembled heart denied
my heart three times again my paltry heart
which knew the names but refused to ask
my heart that hid the answer beneath a stone

my sediment heart that made at last some full confession

from these I turned /

from these saints I turned   these killed kids

                                        these   kids

                      I turned away

too and turned from every prophet

    & the Prophet & the Prophet & the Prophet & the Prophet
    & the Prophet & the Propher & the Prophet & the Prophet
    & the Prophet & the Prophet & the Prophet & the Prophet
    & the Prophet & the Propher & the Prophet & the Prophet
    & the Prophet & the Prophet & the Prophet & the Prophet
    & the Prophet & the Prophet & the Prophet & the Prophet
    & the Prophet & the Prophet & the Prophet & the Prophet
    & the Prophet & the Propher & the Prophet & the Prophet
    & the Prophet & the Prophet & the Prophet & the Prophet
    & the Prophet & the Prophet & the Prophet & the Prophet
    & the Prophet & the Propher & the Prophet & the Prophet
    & the Prophet & the Prophet & the Prophet & the Prophet
    & the Prophet & the Propher & the Prophet & the Prophet
    & the Prophet & the Prophet & the Prophet & the Prophet

              ...& & &...

what hearts   I shattered

what mothers   I shattered

what homes what names I shattered

                              if I remember it all // write every all

   it will not be   unshattered

cannot   be   unshattered

if I hope

to ever be

better

than I am

have been

to ever rise

unwinged

but graced

if I hope

to ever

unshatter

ora pro nobis ora pro me ora pro nobis ora pro me

88

some poems

Manmade water

The weather was long and clattered. I guess there were clouds.
And wind from one way to the next. Good birds filled their bones
With air and made romance with bad birds. Bad birds dropped
Stitches above the river and called foul. Hunger left a mark
On my lowest incisor. I unmeant the line about birds. Stated clouds
As corollary for possible rain. Intentional flood. I bit through
The branch closest to the banks. Beneath the water. Above the other
Water. Redacted birds threw halos to the flood mark. I parlayed
Stones. Made query of the fence line. In diamond sutured drops
Of unproven rain. I made clatter. And then unmade clatter.
The weather grew shutters. Closed itself off from theoretical names.
It called itself hunger. I believed every word. Made elegant maps
To guide myself through fog. I counted every tooth from everything

Broken. I scratched out my letters and
                                  unlearned the reason for wet.

The gospel writers

A boy raised sticks to a yielding sky. Magiced holes into blacker holes.
As bones filled themselves with feathers. Along the palimpsest pulse
There was the promise of soil. There were lines about wires. Signal bent
By light arcing low across the third horizon. I erased them all. Wrote
Instead of the girl without wings whose skin split the skull of a plaited
Song. A vibrating string. Whose hands held nothing because she held
No hands. Held in their place the hollow thump of blood. Of bandages
Wrapped and wound by the tension of wind. I removed my last tongue
And tacked it taut to the firebound tree. Crumpled every creasing sound
That ever cracked across my teeth and replaced them with the great
And heaving weight of nothing. I swallowed an empty sky and belched
Forth stars. Remembered the rood. A fearsome boy. An unfalling girl.
Their brown faces blessing the burden of stones with impossible names.

I cut my pens and scratched their signs

                                        as hope into my palm's sacrad heart.

Unwritten & open letters to Jack Christian

I put my shoulder to it. The weak one with a pinktoothed skull
Leaned awhile above or let's call it near a chumbellied robin taught
To breathe fire. I said to maybe let me implore like what I tell is wager.
The subtle implication of wet on wet. If time is an unmeant thing
And you wrote in such tall letters then what. They were still orange
And what I was was nervous. And orange was really to be read
Perhaps simply as scribble over. It was midnight or whenever
Because which facts we previously established by joint decree.
When we called to order a congress of hurt we passed a motion
To ask the blinds raised. Which is to say unbeige beige. Someone
Once opined that beige was like to invisible or maybe the word
Was calm. The window faced north which we understood to be good
For our art. It was whatever if ever what was ever ever.

Which we knew in our hearts to be false
                                        nothing being such as never again.

Make or break Star City

Remember that season we gathered without shadow.
Got rowdy and filled the creek with cuss. There were two beards
In the trash and nothing was new. It was night and that one star
Was the only same again thing. Or maybe just the only thing
Worth carving to what mountain. You were sleeping that one time
I sneaked down three stairs to unsense the sound of meaning. I meant
Meaning writ large. As if words themselves were mere as bells to decorate
The fugit-ness of time. That was so many administrations ago. The only
Pundit left we can trust is the river. Every other channel scrabbled static.
A nonbreeze blew through passably brown branches. If I had wanted
To wake you I didn't know it. Going back to that one line about sleeping.
Referring back to that sense of sneaking through a duskdrawn house.
In search of some shape to wrap my lazy mouth around. In hard want

Of some sound to know by which I mean

                                        of course I miss you buddy.

Drumbelly gnosis

Someone scraped red across the sky. My tongue broke blue
Like painted bone. I maybe meant those sparks in my maybe throat.
Black birds bent from flight stitched a sigh through leafbright branches.
There were eyes behind my other eyes. My new and brightest eyes.
I slacked the wire between my thoughts and jaw. Unhinged a sign trained
By teeth. Wind shook water into shapes of prayer as blacker birds lapsed
A brittle shine. There was time but what was it. Praise but who for. I unmeant
Who and directed the object to whom. But whom for. Lonely dogs circled
Blackest birds. Whose beaks broke news of future angels. Whose hollow
Bones slowly filled with glue. Someone scratched my secret name onto
The whisper post. Delivered a wing wrapped in twine to my hidden forest.
Weather was a thing that happened. Measured by unsprung clocks powered
By an astronaut's tear. At night I polished my troop of invisible beasts.

I spoke their names in imagined tongues

                                    and meant every terrible sound.

I made for you a new machine and all it does is hope

I made for you a new machine and all it does is hope

I made for you a new machine and all it does is hope

I made for you a new machine and all it does is hope

I made for you a new machine and all it does is hope

I made for you a new machine and all it does is hope

I made for you a new machine and all it does is hope

I made for you a new machine and all it does is hope

I made for you a new machine and all it does is hope

I made for you a new machine and all it does is hope

I made for you a new machine and all it does is hope

I made for you a new machine and all it does is hope

I made for you a new machine and all it does is hope

I made for you a new machine and all it does is hope

I made for you a new machine and all it does is hope

notes on the text

psallite sapienter has been variously translated as "sing and play," "sing wisely," and "sing praise with all your skill," to cite just a few.

"ten thousand psalms" contains allusions, however adjacent, to the following: the King James Bible; the Latin Vulgate; Cicero; Wittgenstein's "Blue" and "Brown" books; St. Juan de la Cruz; Meister Eckhart; Ralph Waldo Emerson; the *Apophthegmata Patrum*; the Rule of St. Benedict; St. Augustine of Hippo; Hildegard Von Bingen; The Cloud of Unknowing; St. Jane Frances de Chantal; Thomas Merton; Karl Marx; and Saint Teresa of Ávila.

The Washington Post's database of police shootings was regularly consulted during the composition of *confiteor // untitled*, particularly the years 2016 - 2018 during which the poem was written and revised. With shame and humility, please read their names, say their names, and remember their names. We must be better.

about the author

richard lucyshyn lives in Richmond, VA with his family. He currently splits his time teaching poetry and creative writing at The College of William and Mary and being a stay-at-home parent with his young children.

acknowledgements

Humble thanks to the editors of *Gramma*, *Sprung Formal*, *Incessant Pipe*, *Drunk In A Midnight Choir*, and *Reality Beach* for publishing earlier version of some of these poems. A small portion of this book first appeared in the chapbook *Geoffrey Tungsten's Grievesome River*, published by Sybil Press in 2016.

Thank you, Chris Tonelli and Allison Titus, for the patient and generous advice on how to navigate new terrain.

Thank you, Dara Wier, for these many years of steadfast and enthusiastic encouragement.

Thank you to my teachers and confidants, Cathryn Hankla, Jack Christian, and Amanda Petrusich for the unwavering support and thoughtful guidance.

Thank you, Dave Locke, Opie, and my extended family at All For One and Old Glory, including Ben Butts, Joe Nickley, Ryan Bailey, Juicy, Cameron, and Max. You welcomed me into your home and insisted I belong. I am forever in your debt.

Thank you, Slim Spacebird. I am humbled to know you. Thank you, Todd Cocks, for the steadfast encouragement.

Thank you, Adam Tedesco and Amie Zimmerman, for helping me to understand that there is room for me in the poetry world.

Thank you, Elæ {Lynne} and everyone at The Operating System. You are a grace in this world.

Thank you Kelly, Hazel, and Levon. You are my home and hope.

Thank you.
Peace.

'increasing the mass of the world':
a poetics and process conversation
with Richard Lucyshyn and Elæ

Greetings comrade! Thank you for talking to us about your process today! Can you introduce yourself, in a way that you would choose?

Hi hi hi! My name is Richard Lucyshyn, and I live in Richmond, VA with Kelly, my spouse, our two young children, and our two rescued dogs Bunk and Mitch (an albino Pomeranian we literally found wandering down the street by herself). We used to have some cat friends living with us, Milhouse and Ely, but they have both passed. We miss them dearly but are lucky to have shared a world with them for such long times; Milhouse made it to fourteen, and Ely to just shy of thirteen.

Why are you a poet/writer/artist?

Making poems is one of a very places/times where I am able to play with and use language, words and sounds, in the ways that are most natural to me. There is no immediate need or pressure to wrangle myself into an approximate shape of "this is how people communicate and interact with each other."

Perhaps I'll never really be certain, but maybe it really is as simple as that.

When did you decide you were a poet/writer/artist (and/or: do you feel comfortable calling yourself a poet/writer/artist, what other titles or affiliations do you prefer/feel are more accurate)?

Some folks find themselves keen on poems when they're bitty little kids. Some of us don't realize that we're curious until we're older, maybe a lot or maybe a little. As far back as I can remember, I've always been a reader. I read a whole bunch way back then, and I read even more now.

But I think the first time I was hipped to poems other than those things I was taught in school was during my junior (or it might have been senior) year of high school when a friend gifted me a copy of C.K. Wiliams's *Selected Poems*, the one that came out just a few year earlier in 1994. I'm not sure I "liked" it a whole lot back then (nor would I say I "disliked" in any active sense), and I certainly hadn't learned how to read them yet. Luckily I was self-aware just enough to realize that I was looking at poems doing things I hadn't seen done before. At least in what poems I had encountered up to that point. And for whatever confluence of reasons, it was a pretty easy leap for me to make, starting from "well, if that dude can make poems do things I didn't know poems could do" to "gee, I wonder what else poems can do." I've been chasing that tumbleweed ever since; playing with sounds and words and language, trying to figure out how it works and how far I can stretch it before it breaks.

Probably for now I'm going to set aside much discussion of whether I am "comfortable" calling myself a poet. The short answer is no, that my brain locks up when others refer to me, or ask me if I am, a poet. Because my instinctual and gut-determined response is something close to "oh gosh, like, poems are things I make and do sometimes and think about a great deal of time, but I make and do lots and lots of stuff. I make a bunch of mistakes and messes. Also, sandwiches." And I tend to get stuck there, because I don't mean those things in any sort of glib or sarcastic way; I don't mean it to diminish poems and the people who make them, or whoever is asking me if I am or calling me a "poet." Depending on how any particular person or people define, or otherwise conceive, the "idea" of poetry, of what a poet is, my natural response could very well be perceived as disrespectful, as minimizing something hugely important.

It's difficult enough to articulate even in writing, when I have all the time in the world and all the space I might need. Truthfully, I'm still working to figure it all out, and maybe I never will. And that's ok!

Having said all of that, though, I don't take issue with folks if and when they say "Richard is a poet" or whatelse. So, if you don't mind me standing there for a possibly awkward amount of time before I respond when you ask "are you a poet," looking as if I've been overcome with some existential crisis (which in a way it is, because I am in fact reconsidering my identity or what even "identity" is) then we can totally be friends. It's just a thing that happens to me, and that's also ok!

Needless to say, I lead a tremendously rich and exciting inner life.

What's a "poet" (or "writer" or "artist") anyway? What do you see as your cultural and social role (in the literary / artistic / creative community and beyond)?

I'm most soothed by the functional sense that a poet is just a mind that makes a poem or maybe even makes lots of them. However they feel a poem can or should be made. In whatever form they think a poem can or should take at any time.

I've never found any treasure in the idea that in order to make a poem a person must have some special whatevers. Or that they must be maybe tuned with any magic everythings.

Which is not at all to say that poems can't be magic. Probably most of them aren't, but plenty of folks know know and trust that some of them are. And how much more beautiful is it that those poems - or paintings or songs or you-make-its - that are magic were made by any old so and so.

There's grace and hope in that. Maybe it's so much than that, and that's what hope and grace are.

Dollars to doughnuts, when some particular anybody makes a serious attempt at the project of poem-making, consciously or not they are trying to make a poem that is necessary. Or that was always "supposed" to exist but, for reasons, just hasn't been born yet. Something was missing and then it wasn't. And then everything is different. Like, everything in the sense of every thing ever. The impact or size of that change doesn't really matter a lick, I don't think. A poem could be read by/connect to millions of people or three. Or one. The change still happens.

And that's so rad! That we can increase the mass of the world just by figuring out how to make something it was always meant to have. That anyone can do it if or because they feel like it.

I don't know, but that seems pretty darn special to me.
Talk about the process or instinct to move these poems (or your work

in general) as independent entities into a body of work. How and why did this happen? Have you had this intention for a while? What encouraged and/or confounded this (or a book, in general) coming together? Was it a struggle?

I spent the last 13 or 14 years, ermmmm, trying to teach myself to learn how to make the poems I had "in my head" but hadn't seen before. Somewhere about 2 1/2 years ago, plus or minus some change, I noticed I was making those poems. Or really, that I was about as close as I was likely ever going to get.

What does your title represent? How was it generated? Talk about the way you titled the book, and how your process of naming (individual pieces, sections, etc) influences you and/or colors your work specifically.

The title "I made for you a new machine and all it does is hope" actually evolved out of a small painting I had made a year or three before most of the book had even been written. A recurring image I sometimes or often return to in my visual practice, paintings or drawings that are actually just poems meant to be looked at, is a creaky tripod like structure (like, maybe picture the offspring of a giant pyramid mated to some scaffolding) that is often (except when it isn't) broadcasting light or color or sound from its peak. Anyway, I made, gave away, and subsequently totally forgot about one of these paintings on which I had also written "I BUILT A MACHINE AND ALL IT DOES IS HOPE."

Cut to a year or two later when I was shining the manuscript up, getting it ready to send out. I shared it along to an old and dear friend of mine to give it a read and some thoughts so that I could gauge if the poems were doing what I trying to make them do and, if so, how well. I had slapped "A Newly Book of Uncommon Prayer" (or something in that neighborhood anyway) on as a title not so long before, thinking it would get the job done. But I was never really committed to it.

A couple or few weeks later, my pal got back to me with a small handful of suggestions. One of which was basically "dig…that title is doing either too much work or not nearly enough." I was instantly like "yup!" His next pro-tip was to think about "I built a machine and all it does is hope," from that painting I was gabbing about a couple or few paragraphs ago. As I mentioned up there, I had forgotten all about it until he poked me in my memory palace.

And it fit. Well nearly fit. It needed to be longer. And to express as a gift which is really a plea. And it needed to be way more iambic which is entirely iambic for no other reason than that's how it's supposed to be.

So it grew itself just a bit into a 7-footed lope. And then it grew itself again into a sonnet sort-of.

All according to plan.

What does this particular work represent to you as indicative of your method/creative practice /history/mission/intentions/hopes/plans?

I can't wrangle together an answer, that feels any way honest, beyond that these were just the poems I was trying to make over those months that I made them. Once I figured them out I felt "oh yeah, these are them I was looking for." And then I was able to stop looking for them quite so hard.

What does this book DO (as much as what it says or contains)?

This book is simply a series of attempts to learn something.

What would be the best possible outcome for this book? What might it do in the world, and how will its presence as an object facilitate your creative role in your community and beyond?

I hope to learn. To have my mistakes and errors and wrongs pointed out to me so that I might listen and learn. And continue always trying to be better than I am.

What are your hopes for this book, and for your practice?

Hope. That's all, really. I hope. And I hope.

Is there anything else we should have asked, or that you want to share?

A good pencil just feels right. And I could talk to you about pencils for longer than you might prefer.

WHY PRINT / DOCUMENT?

The Operating System uses the language "print document" to differentiate from the book-object as part of our mission to distinguish the act of documentation-in-book-FORM from the act of publishing as a backwards-facing replication of the book's agentive *role* as it may have appeared the last several centuries of its history. Ultimately, I approach the book as TECHNOLOGY: one of a variety of printed documents (in this case, bound) that humans have invented and in turn used to archive and disseminate ideas, beliefs, stories, and other evidence of production.

Ownership and use of printing presses and access to (or restriction of printed materials) has long been a site of struggle, related in many ways to revolutionary activity and the fight for civil rights and free speech all over the world. While (in many countries) the contemporary quotidian landscape has indeed drastically shifted in its access to platforms for sharing information and in the widespread ability to "publish" digitally, even with extremely limited resources, the importance of publication on physical media has not diminished. In fact, this may be the most critical time in recent history for activist groups, artists, and others to insist upon learning, establishing, and encouraging personal and community documentation practices. Hear me out.

With The OS's print endeavors I wanted to open up a conversation about this: the ultimately radical, transgressive act of creating PRINT /DOCUMENTATION in the digital age. It's a question of the archive, and of history: who gets to tell the story, and what evidence of our life, our behaviors, our experiences are we leaving behind? We can know little to nothing about the future into which we're leaving an unprecedentedly digital document trail — but we can be assured that publications, government agencies, museums, schools, and other institutional powers that be will continue to leave BOTH a digital and print version of their production for the official record. Will we?

As a (rogue) anthropologist and long time academic, I can easily pull up many accounts about how lives, behaviors, experiences — how THE STORY of a time or place — was pieced together using the deep study of correspondence, notebooks, and other physical documents which are no longer the norm in many lives and practices. As we move our creative behaviors towards digital note taking, and even audio and video, what can we predict about future technology that is in any way assuring that our stories will be accurately told – or told at all? How will we leave these things for the record? In these documents we say:
   WE WERE HERE, WE EXISTED, WE HAVE A DIFFERENT STORY

- Elæ [Lynne DeSilva-Johnson], Founder/Creative Director
THE OPERATING SYSTEM, Brooklyn NY 2018

2019

Ark Hive-Marthe Reed
I Made for You a New Machine and All it Does is Hope - Richard Lucyshyn
Illusory Borders-Heidi Reszies
A Year of Misreading the Wildcats - Orchid Tierney
The Suitcase Tree - Filip Marinovich
We Are Never The Victims - Timothy DuWhite
Of Color: Poets' Ways of Making | An Anthology of Essays on Transformative Poetics -
Amanda Galvan Huynh & Luisa A. Igloria, Editors

KIN(D)* Texts and Projects

A Bony Framework for the Tangible Universe-D. Allen
Opera on TV-James Brunton
Hall of Waters-Berry Grass
Transitional Object-Adrian Silbernagel

Glossarium: Unsilenced Texts and Translations

Śnienie / Dreaming - Marta Zelwan/Krystyna Sakowicz, (Poland, trans. Victor Miluch)
Alparegho: Pareil-À-Rien / Alparegho, Like Nothing Else - Hélène Sanguinetti (France, trans. Ann Cefola)
High Tide Of The Eyes - Bijan Elahi (Farsi-English/dual-language)
trans. Rebecca Ruth Gould and Kayvan Tahmasebian
 In the Drying Shed of Souls: Poetry from Cuba's Generation Zero
Katherine Hedeen and Víctor Rodríguez Núñez, translators/editors
Street Gloss - Brent Armendinger with translations for Alejandro Méndez, Mercedes Roffé, Fabián Casas, Diana Bellessi, and Néstor Perlongher (Argentina)
Operation on a Malignant Body - Sergio Loo (Mexico, trans. Will Stockton)
Are There Copper Pipes in Heaven - Katrin Ottarsdóttir
(Faroe Islands, trans. Matthew Landrum)

2018

An Absence So Great and Spontaneous It Is Evidence of Light - Anne Gorrick
The Book of Everyday Instruction - Chloë Bass
Executive Orders Vol. II - a collaboration with the Organism for Poetic Research
One More Revolution - Andrea Mazzariello
Chlorosis - Michael Flatt and Derrick Mund
Sussuros a Mi Padre - Erick Sáenz
Sharing Plastic - Blake Nemec
In Corpore Sano : Creative Practice and the Challenged Body [Anthology]
Abandoners - L. Ann Wheeler
Jazzercise is a Language - Gabriel Ojeda-Sague
Born Again - Ivy Johnson
Attendance - Rocío Carlos and Rachel McLeod Kaminer
Singing for Nothing - Wally Swist
The Ways of the Monster - Jay Besemer
Walking Away From Explosions in Slow Motion - Gregory Crosby
Field Guide to Autobiography - Melissa Eleftherion

Glossarium: Unsilenced Texts and Translations

The Book of Sounds - Mehdi Navid (Farsi dual language, trans. Tina Rahimi
Kawsay: The Flame of the Jungle - María Vázquez Valdez
(Mexico, trans. Margaret Randall)
Return Trip / Viaje Al Regreso - Israel Dominguez; (Cuba, trans. M.Randall)

for our full catalog please visit:
https://squareup.com/store/the-operating-system/

*deeply discounted Book of the Month and Chapbook Series subscriptions
are a great way to support the OS's projects and publications!*
sign up at: http://www.theoperatingsystem.org/subscribe-join/

DOC U MENT
/däkyəmənt/

First meant "instruction" or "evidence," whether written or not.

noun - a piece of written, printed, or electronic matter that provides information or evidence or that serves as an official record
verb - record (something) in written, photographic, or other form
synonyms - paper - deed - record - writing - act - instrument

[*Middle English, precept, from Old French, from Latin documentum, example, proof, from docre, to teach; see dek- in Indo-European roots.*]

Who is responsible for the manufacture of value?

Based on what supercilious ontology have we landed in a space where we vie
against other creative people in vain pursuit of the fleeting credibilities
of the scarcity economy, rather than freely collaborating
and sharing openly with each other in ecstatic celebration of MAKING?

While we understand and acknowledge the economic pressures and fear-monger
that threatens to dominate and crush the creative impulse, we also believe that
now more than ever we have the tools to relinquish agency via cooperative mea
fueled by the fires of the Open Source Movement.

**Looking out across the invisible vistas of that rhizomatic parallel country
we can begin to see our community beyond constraints, in the place
where intention meets resilient, proactive, collaborative organization.**

Here is a document born of that belief, sown purely of imagination and will.
When we document we assert. We print to make real, to reify our being there.
When we do so with mindful intention to address our process, to open our wor
to others, to create beauty in words in space, to respect and acknowledge
the strength of the page we now hold physical, a thing in our hand,
we remind ourselves that, like Dorothy: *we had the power all along, my dears.*

THE PRINT! DOCUMENT SERIES
is a project of
the trouble with bartleby
in collaboration with
the operating system

I MADE FOR
rich
YOU A NEW
a r d l.
ACHINE A
l u c y
DALL IT DO
s h y n
ES IS HOPE

www.ingramcontent.com/pod-product-compliance
Lightning Source LLC
Chambersburg PA
CBHW030119100526
44591CB00009B/459